INDIA'S GREAT PERSONALITY

VAIDIK JINJALA

Made with ♥ on the Notion Press Platform
www.notionpress.com

Contents

Mahatma Gandhi

Mahatma Gandhi

Mohandas Karamchand Gandhi (Mahatma Gandhi) was born on October 2, 1869, into a Hindu Modh family in Porbanadar, Gujarat, India. His father, named Karamchand Gandhi, was the Chief Minister (diwan) of the city of Porbanadar. His mother, named Putlibai, was the fourth wife; the previous three wives died in childbirth. Gandhi was born into the vaishya (business caste). He was 13 years old when married Kasturbai (Ba) Makhanji, through his parents arrangement. They had four sons. Gandhi learned tolerance and non-injury to living beings from an early age. He was abstinent from meat, alcohol, and promiscuity.

Gandhi studied law at the University of Bombay for one year, then at the University College London, from which he graduated in 1891, and was admitted to the bar of England. His reading of "Civil Disobedience" by David Thoreau inspired his devotion to the principle of non-violence. He returned to Bombay and practiced law there for a year, then went to South Africa to work for an Indian firm in Natal. There Gandhi experienced racism: he was thrown off a train while holding a valid first class ticket and pushed to third class. Later he was beaten by a stagecoach driver for refusing to travel on the foot-board to make room for a European passenger. He was barred from many hotels because of his race. In 1894, Gandhi founded the Natal Indian Congress. They focused on the Indian cause and British discrimination in South Africa. In 1897, Gandhi brought his wife and children to South Africa. He was attacked by a mob of racists, who tried to lynch him. He refused to press charges on any member of the mob. Gandhi became the first non-white lawyer to be admitted to the bar in South Africa.

India won independence in 1947, followed by the Indo-Pakistani War of 1947, and partition of India. Gandhi said,

"Before partitioning India, my body will have to be cut into two pieces." About one million people died in the bloody riots until partition was reluctantly asserted by Gandhi as the only way to stop the Civil War. He urged the Congress Party to accept partition, and launched his last "fast-into-death" campaign in Delhi, calling for a stop to all violence. Gandhi also called to give Pakistan the 550,000,000 rupees in honor of the partition agreement. He tried to prevent instability and anger against India.

Gandhi was shot three times in the chest and died while on his way to a prayer meeting, on January 30, 1948. His assassins were convicted and executed a year later. The ashes of Mahatma Gandhi were split in portions and sent to all states of India to be scattered in rivers. Part of Gandhi's ashes rest in Raj Ghat, near Delhi, India. Part of Mahatma Gandhi's ashes are at the Lake Shrine in Los Angeles.
Steve Shelokhonov

APJ Abdul Kalam

A.P.J Abdul kalam

Great personalities are not born every day; they are born once in a century and are remembered for millennialsto come. One such great personality that we will always be proud of is Dr. APJ Abdul Kalam. His full name was Avul Pakir Jainulabdeen Abdul Kalam, born in Rameswaram of Madras Presidency on 15th October 1931 and died on July 27, 2015, Shillong. He was an Indian Scientist and also a politician leader, who later became the 11th President of India. He played an important role in the development of India's missile and nuclear weapons program.

Dr. A P J Abdul Kalam was born to a poor Tamil Muslim family. He lived with his family in the temple city of Tamilnadu, Rameswaram, where his father, Jainulabdeen, had a boat and was an imam of a local mosque. At the same time, his mother, Ashiamma, was a housewife. Kalam had four brothers and one sister in his family, from which he was the youngest. Kalam's ancestors were wealthy traders and landowners and had vast land and property tracts. But with time, their business of ferrying pilgrims and trading groceries suffered huge losses due to the Pamban Bridge's opening. As a result, Kalam's family had become inadequate and struggled hard to make a living. At a tender age, Kalam had to sell newspapers to supplement his family income.

Sir Kalam was entitled to be the 11th president of India. His term period of 25th July 2002 to 25th July 2007 was achieved by winning a presidential election in 2002 with a massive margin of votes. National Democratic Alliances' nominated him to be president and it was supported by Samajwadi Party and National Congress Party. He was lovingly called as peoples' president as he had done uncountable works for the welfare of the people and through the entire country.

He was brave and courageous enough to take decisions and implement them no matter if that was tough or sensitive or highly controversial. The "office of profit" is perhaps the hard Act that he had to sign. The "office of profit", according to the English Act of Settlement in 1701 explains that no single individual who has a professional set up under the royal family, who has some kind of provision with or who is taking a pension from the prince has the right to work for the of the "House of Commons". This will allow the royal family to have zero influence on the administrative conditions.

He had also become one of the most talked-about presidents Rule in 2005 for imposing the Presidents' rule in Bihar. Kalam expressed his wish to take up the position one more time but then later changed his mind.

After taking farewell from the office, he shifted and commenced his career as a visiting professor at the Indian Institute of Management in Shillong. He served as an Aerospace Engineering professor at Anna University, Tamil Nadu. He also lit up educational institutions like the Indian Institute of Indore, Indian Institute of Bangalore with his presence and knowledge. Sir Kalam served as chancellor Indian Institute of Space Science and Technology, Thiruvananthapuram.

In 2012, he introduced a program called "What Can I Give?" focusing on the theme of eradicating corruption from the country.

CHAPTER THREE

Bhagat Singh

Bhagat Singh

Bhagat Singh was born on September 27, 1907, in the village of Banga near Lyallpur district in Punjab, British India. He was an Indian freedom fighter who is considered to be one of the most influential revolutionaries of the Indian independence movement. Bhagat Singh joined the Hindustan Republican Association (HRA) at a young age and became involved in revolutionary activities. He participated in several acts of sabotage against British institutions, including an attempt to bomb the Central Legislative Assembly in Delhi. In 1929, he and two other activists were convicted of assassinating John Saunders, a British police officer. Singh was executed by hanging on March 23, 1931, at Lahore jail at the age of 23. Despite his short life, Bhagat Singh left a lasting legacy in the struggle for Indian independence. He is revered by many as a martyr and symbol of resistance to British colonialism in India. His example continues to inspire new generations of activists worldwide.

Bhagat Singh's life is an inspiration to all those who fight for justice and against oppression. He was a brave young man who dedicated his life to the struggle for Indian independence. His story is a reminder that even in the face of great adversity, it is possible to achieve victory. Bhagat Singh's biography provides insight into the mind of a revolutionary and offers encouragement to those who are fighting for change today. It is an important read for anyone interested in history, politics, or human rights activism. He was loved and respected by the people of India, who continue to honor his memory.

Bhagat Singh's biography covers his upbringing in Punjab, his involvement with revolutionary groups throughout his teenage years, and the significant impact he had on India's struggle for independence. It details his trial when he was charged with the murder of John P. Saunders, a British police officer, as well as his life in prison leading up to his execution at Lahore jail when he was 23 years old. Throughout it all, Bhagat Singh remained strong in defense of Indian independence even in the face of great adversity.

Bhagat Singh's biography is both informative and entertaining to read; full of events that shaped him into becoming an influential figure during India's push for independence from British rule. While it is useful for researchers and historians, anyone interested in politics or Indian history can benefit from reading an in-depth account of the life of a revolutionary icon whose passion lives on through his legacy and impact on India's independence movement.

CHAPTER FOUR

Satyendra Nath Bose

Satyendra Nath Bose

Satyendra Nath Bose, was born on 1st January, 1894, Calcutta (now Kolkata), India. Satyendra Nath Bose was Mathematician and physicist from India known for his work with Albert Einstein on a theory about the gaslike properties of electromagnetic radiation. Satyendra Nath Bose passed away in Calcutta on February 4, 1974.

During his time in high school and college, Satyendra Nath Bose was a brilliant student. In all of his exams, including those for his graduate and post-graduate degrees, he scored in first position. He passed with a M.Sc. in mixed mathematics from the Presidency College in Calcutta in the year 1915, first taught at the University of Dacca (1921–45), then returned to Calcutta (1945–56). Satyendra Nath Bose produced numerous scientific publications between 1918 and 1956 that advanced statistical mechanics, the understanding of the ionosphere's electromagnetic properties, the theories of X-ray crystallography and thermo luminescence, and unification field theory. After reading his Planck's Law and the Hypothesis of Light Quanta (1924), Einstein asked Bose for cooperation.

Satyendra Nath Bose began working as a Reader in Physics at the then-new Dacca University in 1921. He wrote a paper to derive Planck's Law when he was lecturing. Planck's Law and Light Quantum Hypothesis was the title of his paper. Light is released in discrete amounts (quanta) rather than as a continuous wave, Max Planck had explained in the theory of black body radiation in 1900. He derived this formula, but other scientists, including him, did not find it adequate. Later, in a study published in 1905, Albert Einstein provided an explanation of the photoelectric phenomenon based on Planck's quanta as photons. Not for his works on relativity, but for this article, Einstein received the Nobel Prize.

However, many of his colleagues did not share his complete conviction in his as-yet-undeveloped photon theory. Satyendra Nath Bose sent Albert Einstein the article again in June 1924 under these conditions, pleading earnestly for him to read it. Einstein understood the importance of this paper right away. His idea of the photoelectric effect was going to be supported and revolutionized by this study. Einstein himself translated Satyendra Nath Bose's paper into German and sent it to Zeitschrift für Physik with his endorsement for publication. Einstein spoke with great authority due to his standing as a demigod. Bose quickly gained national attention after it was quickly published.

On 4 June 2022, Google honored Bose by featuring him on a Google Doodle marking the 98th anniversary of Satyendra Nath Bose sending his quantum formulations to the German scientist Albert Einstein It was acknowledged as a key quantum mechanical discovery by Albert Einstein.

CHAPTER FIVE

C.V.Raman

C.V Raman

Chandrasekhara Venkata Raman was born on November 7, 1888 in the city of Trichinopoly, Madras Presidency, British India. Today the city is known as Tiruchirappalli and sits in the Indian state of Tamil Nadu.

Raman's father was Chandrasekaran Ramanathan Iyer, a teacher of mathematics and physics. His mother was Parvathi Ammal, who was taught to read and write by her husband. At the time of Raman's birth, the family lived on a low income. Raman was the second of eight children.

Raman's family were Brahmins, the Hindu caste of priests and scholars. His father, however, paid little attention to religious matters: Raman grew up to share his father's casual attitude to religion, but he did observe some Hindu rituals culturally and respected traditions such as vegetarianism.

n 1903, aged just 14, Raman set off for the great city of Madras (now Chennai) to live in a hostel and begin a bachelor's degree at Presidency College. When Raman returned home after his first year at college, his parents were shaken by his unhealthy appearance. They set up a house for him in Madras, where he could be looked after by his grandparents.

Raman was enormously enthusiastic about science. On vacations he would demonstrate experiments to his younger brothers and sisters.

He completed his degree in 1904, winning medals in physics and English. His British lecturers encouraged him to study for a master's degree in the United Kingdom. Madras's civil surgeon, however, told him that his health was not robust enough to withstand the British climate; he advised Raman to stay in India.

Raman was awarded a scholarship and he remained at Presidency College to study for his master's degree. His outstanding potential was recognized, and he was given unlimited access to the laboratories, where he pursued investigations of his own design.

In November 1906, aged 18, Raman had his first academic paper published. He had initially given it to one of his professors to read, but the professor had not bothered. Raman sent his paper directly to Philosophical Magazine and it was accepted. Its title was Unsymmetrical diffraction-bands due to a rectangular aperture: it was about the behavior of light.

Although Raman was intent upon a scientific career, his brother persuaded him to take the civil service exams. Civil service jobs were highly paid and Raman's family was deeply in debt.

For 10 years Raman worked as a civil servant in the Indian Finance Department in Calcutta (now Kolkata), rising quickly to a senior position. In his free time he carried out research into the physics of stringed instruments and drums. He did this work at the Indian Association for the Cultivation of Science (IACS).

Raman's part-time research work and his lectures were impressive, establishing his reputation as a highly talented physicist. In 1917, the University of Calcutta sought him out and offered him the Palit Chair of Physics. Although it meant a substantial cut in pay, Raman, now aged 28, accepted – the prospect of devoting all of his time to science was worth more to him than money.

Although it was a research professorship, Raman also chose to give lecture courses: he was an exciting lecturer and he inspired his students.

Sardar Vallabhbhai Patel

Sardar vallabhbhai Patel

Sardar Vallabhbhai Patel Date Of Birth- born on October 31st, 1875Sardar Vallabhbhai Patel Birth Place- Nadiad, under Bombay Presidency in British India, present-day GujaratRoles Taken in his lifetime- Barrister, Freedom fighter, Politician and an ActivistAssociation with Political Party- First Deputy Prime Minister of India, for Indian National Congress PartyAwards Received- Bharat Ratna in the year 1991 received posthumouslyDeath- died on December 15, 1950 Place of Death- at the age of 75 in Bombay, present-day Mumbai. Born to Jhaverbhai Patel and Ladba and being one of six children, he lived a very sheltered life. His was a landowning family who was capable of providing for themselves. Sardar Vallabhbhai's birthplace was Nadiad, which was a part of the Central Gujarat Community Leuva Patel Patidar community.

He was a hard worker, and after his exams, he saved up funds with the aim of attaining a Law degree. He became a barrister after his British Law Education. They became a family of four when his wife Jhaverben gave birth to a daughter and a son in 1903 and 1905 respectively. He and his family were now living in Godhra where he was called to the bar (which means a bar exam which one has to pass to commence the practice of law and argue on behalf of others in the court). He passed his bar exam and practised professionally for many years and became a very skilled lawyer with a good reputation.

During his law study, he lived away from home and his family in England for two years and studied with the help of other lawyers by borrowing books from them. He converted his lack of financial resources into opportunities.

In 1909 when he was questioning a witness in court, he received a written message about his wife's demise who was suffering from the relapse and after-effects of emergency surgery for cancer. And without flinching, Vallabhbhai Patel went on with his case and even won. He never again gave in for marriage and decided to live as a widower. It was his stoic nature that he had built since childhood that has helped him through many such tough situations.

He was focused on making a better place for society to survive and encouraged education when he built a school "Edward Memorial High School" in Borsad, he was the founder and the chairman today is known as Jhaverbhai Dajibhai Patel High School. In 1917 in Ahmedabad, he ran in the election for the Sanitation Commissioner role after a lot of persuasion from his friends and won . He garnered a favourable position and a lot of support from other Congressmen when he demonstrated excellent commitment in convincing the villagers and other civilians to revolt against tax pay. He was elected as the President of the Gujarat Pradesh Congress Committee; in 1920 and offered his services till **1945**.

the years 1948 and 1949, he was awarded many honorary doctorates of law by various universities like Nagpur University, the University of Allahabad and Banaras Hindu University, subsequently from Osmania University and Punjab University.

The recognition and awards did not stop coming even after his death, he was awarded the bharat ratna in 1991.He was a great man and deserved the title of "patron saint of India's civil servants" and the "Iron man of India".

Lal Bahadur Shastri

Lal Bahadur Shastri

Lal Bahadur Shastri was born on October 2, 1904, in Mughalsarai, United Provinces of Agra and Oudh, British India (now Uttar Pradesh). Lal Bahadur Shastri's father was Sharada Prasad Srivastava, who was a school teacher before becoming a clerk in the revenue office at Allahabad. His mother was Ramdulari Devi. He was the second child. to He had an elder sister Kailashi Devi and a younger sister Sundari Devi.

When Lal Bahadur Shastri was six months old, his father died in an epidemic of bubonic plague. Lal Bahadur Shastri and his sisters grew up in the home of his maternal grandfather Munshi Hazari Lal after his father died.

Shastri started his education at the East Central Railway Inter college in Mughalsarai at the age of four, under the tutelage of a maulvi, Budhan Mian. He was a student there until the sixth grade.

Lal Bahadur Shastri began seventh grade at Harish Chandra High School in Varanasi.

Lal Bahadur Shastri married Lalita Devi, a Mirzapur native, on May 16, 1928. Kusum Shastri, Hari Krishna Shastri, Suman Shastri, Anil Shastri, Sunil Shastri, and Ashok Shastri were the couple's four sons and two daughters.

The entire Shastri family continues to participate in social initiatives and is actively involved in shaping relevant forums in India to aid in the country's growth and advancement.

After India's independence, Lal Bahadur Shastri was named Parliamentary Secretary in his home state of Uttar Pradesh. Following Rafi Ahmed Kidwai's departure to become a minister at the centre, he became the Minister of Police and Transport under Govind Ballabh Pant's Chief

Ministership on 15 August 1947. He was the first to name female conductors as Transport Minister.

As the minister in charge of the Police Department, he requested that unruly crowds be dispersed using water jets, which he instructed officers to use instead of lathis. During his time as police minister, he was instrumental in putting an end to communal riots in 1947, as well as mass migration and refugee resettlement.

With Jawaharlal Nehru as Prime Minister, Shastri was appointed General Secretary of the All-India Congress Committee in 1951. He was in charge of the candidate selection process and the direction of advertising and electioneering efforts. He was a key figure in the Congress Party's landslide victories in the Indian general elections of 1952, 1957, and 1962.

Lal Bahadur Shastri was a very simple man who worked for the betterment of the country. When he died, all he left was an old car, which he had bought in instalments from the government. He was a member of the Servants of India Society, which encouraged its members to avoid accumulating private property and instead serve the people in public.

He was the first railway minister to resign as a result of moral obligation after a major train crash. The Lal Bahadur Shastri Biography teaches the moral values adopted by one of the most honest and significant figures and politicians in Indian history.

Lal Bahadur Shastri's death date was 11 January 1966. He died in Tashkent, Uzbekistan, one day after signing a peace treaty ending the 1965 Indo-Pakistan War.

He was hailed as a national hero, and the Vijay Ghat memorial was named after him.

Vikram Sara bhai

Vikram Sara Bhai

On August 12, 1919, Vikram Sarabhai was born in Ahmedabad, India. His full name is Vikram Ambalal Sarabhai and he was the son of Ambalal Sarabhai who was a Gujarati industrialist. Dr. Vikram Ambalal Sarabhai was an Indian physicist and an astronomer who started the space research organization and initiated the nuclear power plant in India. Because of his achievement, he is regarded as the Father of the Indian space program. He was honoured with Padma Bhushan in 1966 and the Padma Vibhushan in 1972. Vikram Sarabhai passed away on December 30, 1971, in Kovalam.

In this article on Vikram Sarabhai biography, we are going to discuss who is Vikram Sarabhai, Vikram Sarabhai education, and the achievements he accomplished throughout his life.

Vikram Sarabhai was born on August 12, 1919, in a Gujarati industrial family. His father's name was Ambalal Sarabhai who was an industrialist, a philanthropist, and the founder of the Sarabhai group of companies. His mother's name was Sarla Devi and he was the Eighth son of Ambalal Sarabhai. In 1942, Vikram Sarabhai married Mrinalini who was a classical dancer by profession. The couple had two children. His daughter's name is Mallika, who went on and became an actress and an activist. His son's name is Kartikeya who is one of the world's leading environmentalist educators and a dedicated community builder, he was awarded the Padma Shri in 2012. During his lifetime, Vikram Sarabhai practised Jainism and had dedicated his life to building the Indian space program and that is why he is called the Father of the Indian space program.

Dr. Vikram Sarabhai is considered the father of the Indian space program. He was a great institution builder and helped in establishing a large number of institutions in diverse fields. After returning from Cambridge in 1947, he requested his friends and family members to help him in opening a research institution near his home in Ahmedabad, thus at the age of only 28, he founded the Physical Research Laboratory (PRL) in Ahmedabad on November 11, 1947.

Vikram Sarabhai came from the famous Sarabhai family who was a major industrialist committed to the Indian Independence movement. Vikram Sarabhai attended the Gujarati college in Ahmedabad to complete his higher studies and after doing so he then took admission to the University of Cambridge in England where in 1940, he gave his final honour exam in the Natural Sciences.

Sarbhai returned to Cambridge post world war 2 to pursue his doctorate and in 1945 he submitted a thesis on "Cosmic Ray Investigation in Tropical Latitudes".

The establishment of the Indian space research organization by Vikram Sarabhai is considered to be his greatest achievement. When he returned to India after completing his Doctorate from Cambridge University in London in 1947, he was able to convince the newly formed independent Indian government of the importance of a space program for a developing country like India. Dr. Sarabhai was also supported by Dr. Homi Jehangir Bhabha who is widely regarded as the father of the Indian nuclear science program. He supported Dr. Sarabhai in setting the first rocket launch station in India. At Thumba near Thiruvananthapuram on the coast of the Arabian sea, the first rocket launch centre was established

The inaugural flight was launched on November 21, 1963, with sodium vapour payload after a remarkable effort in setting up the infrastructure, personnel, communication links, and launch pads.

Vikram Sarabhai worked very passionately to ignite India's first satellite, Aryabhatta but unfortunately, he passed away four years before the launch of the satellite. Dr. Vikram Sarabhai was honoured with Padma Bhushan in 1966 and Padma Vibhushan in 1972 to remember and celebrate his life and the legacy he left behind.